LJ KARERI

INHERITANCE:
AFRICAN LEGACY

IN VERSE, NARRATIVES AND CONTEMPLATIONS

All artwork by SoulAfrik Designs
available for purchase at
soulafrik.com

Copyright 2023 Lj Kareri

Published by
WHISTLETREE MEDIA CO.
BURBANK, CA, 91502
www.whistletreemedia.com
info@whistletreemedia.com

Mom– the best of souls, eternal
Dad– our stealthy creative storm
Kerrie– cherished co-heir, forerunner

Mother Africa– my divine privilege

INTRODUCTION

Within the silent strengths and boisterous rhythms of the African homeland lies a story—an inheritance. Exchanged from generations past, to those now present, and for those yet to be.

This project, *"Inheritance: African Legacy - A Mosaic of Verse, Narratives, and Contemplations,"* is a quest into the soul of Africa, as told through its most primal and elegant form of expression: rhythm in words.

In this collection, Lj Kareri aims to capture the essence of Africa's heart and soul. "Inheritance" weaves together poems, stories and essays that delve deep into the continent's past, explore its present, and dream of its future.

"Inheritance" is a reflection. In every line, a story of Africa - its land, its rhythm, its people. You are invited into this entrancing world where words paint a legacy, where each poem and story is a piece of a larger eternal narrative.

This is Africa, in pure form - raw, and real.

Contents

Introduction 5

ESSENCE

The Seed and Root 13
'being african' 19
'sour & sweet': 22
Africa's Soul 22
'faith' 29
'scroll into history' 33

VISCERA

'scars' 38
'what is peace?' 42
'her pain is deep medicine' 44
'griot' 50
'villainy' 54
'self-compassion' 60

PROGENY

'mother tongue' 66
'male benefactor' 69
'Letter from An Ancestor' 74
"Progeny": An Ancestral Mother's Musings 76

UNBIND

'defense' 80
'memories of revolution' 86
.'stifle' : A Labyrinth of Reflection 93

The "Good African": A Critique	97
Millenia	101
'manifesto'	103
'bonds & visions'	107
'millennia: Africa apologia'	110
'god of death': Africa defiant	116
Luminance	119
'signs from heaven': Africa's Humble Brag	121
'arise'	125
'luminance'	128

FUTURIST

'antiquity: a futuristic descendant'	137
'revolution's song'	143
About Author	145

Savannahs stretch,
Wild, free,
Roaming, breathing, living,
Nature's untamed spirit,
Life.

I

ESSENCE

Africa,
Vast, timeless,
Dancing, dreaming, enduring,
Soul of earth, heart of humanity,
Cradle.

The Seed and Root

In the beginning,
there was a seed.
Deep within the cradle of time,
nestled in the heart of the world,
was Africa.

>The rhythm of the earth pulsed through its veins,
>the sun kissed its golden brow,
>and the stars whispered
>secrets to its night.

Like a giant baobab,
Africa's roots
stretch deep and wide.
They touch
the very core of humanity,
reaching back to the earliest memories of mankind.

>Every footstep,
>every laugh,
>every tear that has ever graced this earth
>finds its origin
>in the heart
>of this ancient land.

In the vast savannahs, the silent stories of ancestors
dance in the winds.
The lion's roar
is but an echo of ancient kings and queens
who once ruled vast empires with wisdom and might.
The gentle hum of the deserts
sings a lullaby of warriors
and poets,
dreamers
and seekers,
who chased horizons and embraced the unknown.

Beneath the shade of mango trees, stories are told.
Stories of resilience,
of love,
of hope.
Tales of journeys
across turbulent seas
and desert sands,
of cultures that thrived,
of languages that painted the air
with poetry and song.

    Here,
    by the fireside,
    we learn that
    to know Africa
    is to know the world.

Yet,
like any seed,
Africa has faced darkness.

From the depths of its soil,
it has felt
the weight of histories
that tried to bury its essence,
to silence its song.

    But seeds,
    by their very nature,
    are resilient.
    They break through the toughest of grounds,
    sprouting,
    growing,
    reaching for the sun.
    And Africa, with its indomitable spirit,
    has shown that
    from darkness
    can come
    the most magnificent of blooms.

The rivers,
winding like veins, carry stories of old and new.
The Nile,
the Congo,
the Zambezi - they whisper tales of civilizations
that rose and fell,
of communities that thrived on their banks,
of the sacred bond between land and water.
These waters,
they carry memories,
dreams,
hopes,
and prayers.

And the mountains,
those ancient sentinels, stand tall,
bearing witness to the passage of time.
Kilimanjaro,
the Atlas,
the Drakensberg - they have seen
kingdoms rise,
cultures meld,
and generations find their voice.

In the bustling cities, the rhythm of Africa beats.
From Cairo
 to Cape Town,
from Dakar
to Nairobi,
the pulse of progress intertwines with the echoes of tradition.
It is a dance of the old and new,
a symphony
of hope and possibility.

Africa,
the seed
and root,
is not just a place. It is a heartbeat,
a soul,
a song.
It is the birthplace of humanity,
the mother of all nations.
And in its embrace,
we find a reminder
that we are, and always will be,
connected
by the threads of ancestry,
history,
and love.

You children of this great continent,
honor its legacy,
cherish its wisdom,
and nurture its future.
For in the seed and root of Africa, we find our own stories,
our own dreams,
our own purpose.

'being african'

Africa's pulse,
rhythm,
and heartbeat
embody its identity
and essence.

    Deeper than skin,
    bigger than borders,
    larger than languages
    and tribes.

It is the curious eyes of a child,
the protective lap of a mother,
the cradle embrace of a continent,
and
the guiding hand of a father,
all coming together
a symphony,
existence.

Being African is
to hear
the wisdom of the mountains
that have watched over us for millennia,
to feel
the passion of the rivers
as they carve their legacy,
and to know
the stories the earth tells
when the rains kiss her.

      It is to carry within one's soul
      the echoes of ancestors,
      their dreams,
      their struggles,
      their triumphs.

This essence
 is not merely in the
vast landscapes
or the
riches of cultures,
but in the
everyday moments:
the shared
laughter,
the communal
meals,
the stories
told under the blanket of stars.
It is the spirit, Ubuntu,
the profound recognition
that we are,
because you are;
that our individual essences
are threads
in the grand communal soul.

To embrace one's African essence is
to understand
the depth
of one's roots,
the strength
that comes from unity, and
the beauty
that comes from diversity.

  It is to wear one's identity
  with pride,
  not as a badge,
  but as a radiant cloak
  woven
  from threads of
  history,
  resilience,
   Innovation,
   and love.

Because every African
has within them the essence
of a continent,
a treasure trove of life experiences,
and a testament to the resilient spirit of a people
who have experienced
both great joys
and profound sorrows in their existence—yet
have continued
 to rise,
shine,
and radiate
their
unmatched light
towards
the world.

'sour & sweet': Africa's Soul

A story has been told
for as long as people can remember.
It takes place
in Africa,
known as
the "cradle of the world."

    It is a tale of emotions, those unseen forces
    that have the power
    to move mountains within our souls.
    And in Africa, as I've come to learn,
    emotions
    can be found
     in both
    sweet and sour shades.

The sour is tasted
in the tears
of mothers
who have buried their sons,
the sting
of colonial scars that still burn,
and the pain
of dreams deferred by circumstances
both cruel
and unyielding.

The sourness
is the sharp bite of histories
written by others,
a tale told by invaders,
where Africa is portrayed
as a wild, dark expanse,
waiting,
almost pleading,
to be tamed,
civilized.

    It is the bitter aftertaste
    of having one's narrative subverted
    by the outside world
    and then
        having to reclaim it.

But then,
with the same intensity,
or perhaps
 even greater,
comes the sweet.

    This is the honeyed laughter
    of children playing in the red soils,
    the passionate songs
    that echo across valleys and mountains,
    the diverse array of cultures,
    languages,
    and stories
    that are the wealth of the continent.

The sweetness
 is love—the deep kind of love
that holds communities together
and renders them
impervious
to even
the most violent storms.

We witness it in the stories
we tell each other
that have been passed down through the generations,
the meals we share,
and the dances we perform.

There's a delicate dance in Africa
between these two sensations,
a balance
that might be described as
'...the fine line
between love
and pain'.
For in loving deeply,
one opens oneself
to the potential
of profound hurt.

Yet, it's this very vulnerability
 that makes our African spirit so resilient.

To have known pain and yet choose hope,
to have tasted bitterness
and still savor the sweet moments
- that's the beauty of this emotional palette.

James Baldwin wrote,
"Not everything that is faced can be changed,
 but nothing can be changed until it is faced."

    And in this vast continent,
    our people face their emotions
    with a bravery that is both
    heartbreaking and inspiring.

We do not shy away
from the sour,
nor take the sweet
for granted.
Instead, we work to embrace
the full spectrum,
understanding that life,
in its essence,
is a mix of both.

    The African heart,
    in its boundless depth and resilience,
    recognizes that the sour moments
    make
    the sweet ones
    even more precious.

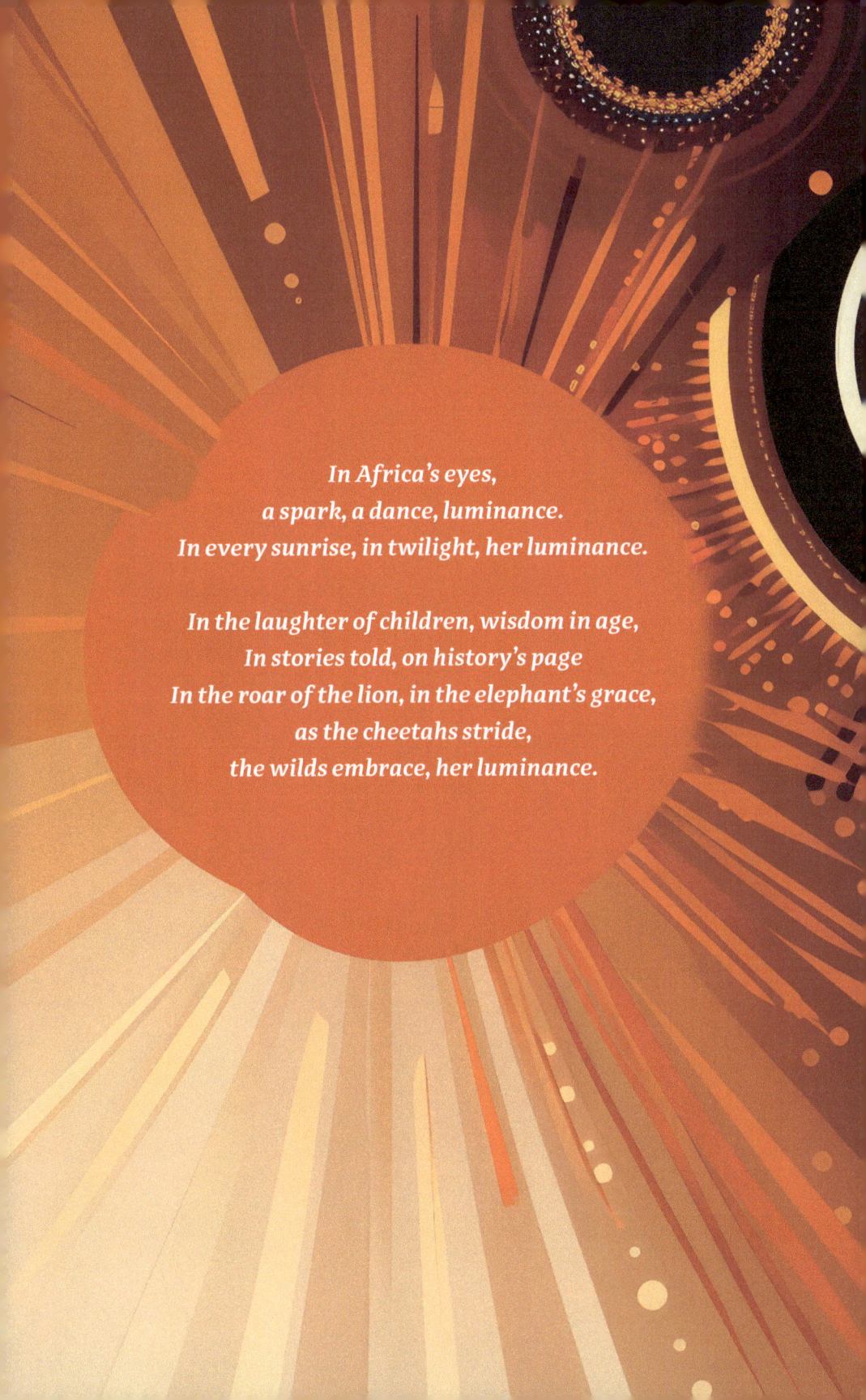

In Africa's eyes,
a spark, a dance, luminance.
In every sunrise, in twilight, her luminance.

In the laughter of children, wisdom in age,
In stories told, on history's page
In the roar of the lion, in the elephant's grace,
as the cheetahs stride,
the wilds embrace, her luminance.

When life demands too much,
Africa stands
 as a symbol.
A quiet power that shines
like a beacon.
Her everlasting faith,
connecting
her past and her present.

To the African man who works the soil,
As your hands bear
the heavy weight of a generational trust,
Consider the ancients, who too gazed at the stars
while uncertain of tomorrow, bearing similar scars.
Yet, it was faith, a quiet affirmation,
that guided their hand.
A belief that their struggles
were part of some grander plan.

To the African woman
who nurtures the flame,
Preserving traditions and giving futures a name:
In the silent moments,
when doubts
cloud your sight,
Reflect on the endless cycle of day into night.
Even the sun,
with its radiant might,
Faces moments of darkness, devoid of its light.
But faith,
in its essence,
is that inner song
Which assures us that night, no matter how long,
gives way to the dawn.

        To the African youth,
        the future's promising seed,
        Bearing dreams
         and hopes,
        and a world to lead:
        Know this, the path ahead
        is not always clear,
        And the voyage of life is oft filled with fear.
        But faith
        is not about clarity,
        or guarantees to be given,
         It's the compass within, when the way isn't driven.
        It's the belief
        in oneself,
        in the Spirit's deep core,
        That
        despite life's uncertainties,
        there's always
        something more.

      Faith, for the everyday African,
      is neither mere trust nor creed,
      It is the lifeblood,
      the essence,
      the deeply-rooted seed.

In a land where promises often seem frail,
Where hope
is a journey,
and resilience the trail,
Faith
stands
as a fortress,
a sanctuary true,
A testament to the spirit, the African hue.

      In our meditations, let us
      dwell on this gift,
      The power
      of faith,
      to uplift
      and to shift.

For in this vast universe, as mysteries unfold,
It is faith
that gives strength,
making the meek
bold.

'scroll into history'

Africa is mysterious
and perplexing.
An ever-changing mosaic
of stories, dreams, and memories
through the twisting alleys of history,
where myths
are entwined with reality.
The stories of its people, stories of faith that are
both intricate and fundamental,
pulsate throughout the continent.

Take the farmer, with his hands marred by the red clay of the earth.
Every time he digs his fingers into the ground,
he transforms into a living link between different eras.
He is speaking to millennia of history:
old kingdoms,
colonial invaders,
 dreams dashed and relinquished.
Despite the din, a single voice emerges,
a whisper
encouraging him
to hope and persevere.
It is a faith
that started long before him.

Then there is the urban woman, navigating vast cities
caught between
tradition and modernity.
The pressure of societal expectations,
the ambitions
she dares to pursue,
and the battles
she fights in silence
are what
bind her life together.
And in the maze that is her heart,
she finds
a strand of faith.
Not the kind found in ancient scrolls,
but the faith
of a woman rewriting
her own
story,
her own
destiny.

The restless and audacious youth stands at the crossroads of the past and the future.
Theirs is a paradoxical world,
split between virtual and physical realities.
However, deep within their search,
amid the cacophony
of revolution and change,
a ring of faith appears. A faith that is neither archaic nor futuristic
but is etched
in the very essence
of their being.

Our lives, are stories that frequently mix
real life events
with made-up narratives.

      In Africa's grand story, faith becomes an elusive character,
      sometimes a hero,
      sometimes a trickster,
      but always present.

It is more than just faith in the unseen; it is faith
 in the story yet to be told,
the chapter yet to be written.
Because in Africa, where history, culture, and beliefs are all
intertwined,
are piled one upon the other,
faith does not look like something from the past;
it looks like the ink
that will write the future.

      It will always stand as a testament
      to the power of stories,
      the magic of myths,
       and the resilience
      of the people of this continent.

II

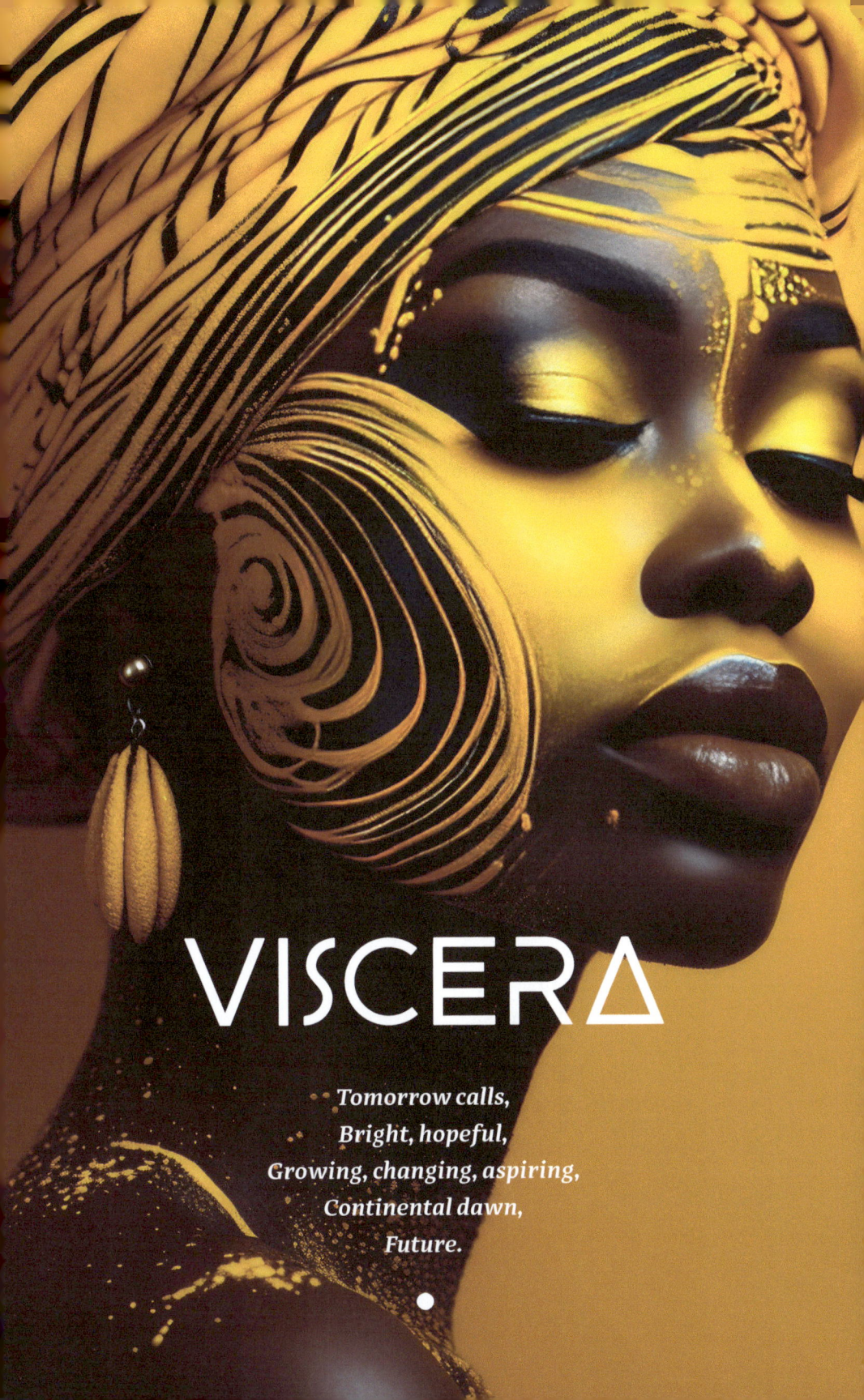

'scars'

In Africa,
where the earth whispers
secrets to those who listen,
there lies a crown,
not of jewels and gold,
but of scars.
Each scar a story,
a fragment of history,
etched into
the very skin of the land and its people.
This is no ordinary crown; it is
a manifest of survival, woven
with threads of
 resilience
and courage.

Africa's scars, a living, breathing testament to
 the continent's tumultuous journey. Each scar,
a narrative
spun from the loom of time,
tells of
empires rising and falling, of
colonial chains broken by
the unyielding spirit of freedom fighters, of
cultures clashing and blending into
a vibrant kaleidoscope.

These scars, they are
not mere blemishes; they are
brushstrokes of history on
the pages of a continent.
They speak of
battles fought, of
tears shed, of
laughter that echoed through the
savannahs and jungles.
They are
the silent witnesses to
the longevity of a people who have
weathered storms and emerged,
not unscathed,
but undefeated.

In the bustling markets, where
life thrums with
an unending rhythm,
in the quiet villages where
ancient wisdom is
passed down through generations,
in the laughter of children, the
hope of the future, these scars are revered.
They are not reminders of a wounded past but
symbols of a future forged with
the will of a people who
refuse to
be defined
by their trials.

Imagine these scars as magical,
glowing lines that
map out the destiny of
a continent reborn
from the ashes of its history. In them
lies the magic of Africa,
an enchantment
 born of
endurance and hope,
a spell
of strength that
no adversity can break.
So
let Africa wear its crown of scars with pride,
for in them lies
the beauty of its soul,
the story of
a rebirth,
a renewal,
a rising.
These scars are
the jewels in Africa's crown, shining
not with the light of pain, but
with the brilliance
of a spirit that
no force on earth can ever diminish.
They are the legacy of
a past
that has shaped
an unbreakable future,
a testament to the fact that
even in scars,
there is beauty,
there is strength,
there is Africa.

'what is peace?'

Peace isn't just the quiet, it's
the spirit unbowed.
It's the songs of
our ancestors, echoing through time,
The tales they told, mountains they'd climb.
It's the gaze
that meets another, without fear or disdain,
The unity
in suffering,
the strength
in shared pain.

>It's the voice that
>dares to challenge, the status quo of old,
>The fire that
>burns fiercely, stories yet untold.

It's in every
whispered secret of lovers under a tree,
In the
shared dreams of freedom, what we strive to be.
It's the passion in the protest,
the love that seeks to heal,
The cry for justice,
the rawness we feel.

It's not just the ceasefire, or
the treaty signed in ink,
But the
mending of broken spirits,
the missing link.

    It's in
    the voice
    of a generation, seeking to break out.

So, when you ask
of peace, in this turbulent time,
Know
it's not just the silence, but
a mountain we climb.

    For peace is
    the fight,
    the struggle,
    the plea,
    The dream
    we hold onto, of
    what the world could be.

'her pain is deep medicine'

She stands as
an embodiment of profound endurance.
Her narrative is not merely one of
beauty and ancient wisdom,
but also of
wounds and scars,
each telling tales
of pain,
resilience,
and rebirth.

> Africa's anguish,
> deeply etched in the annals of time, has
> been both
> a lament
> and a lesson.
> From the shackles of slavery, where
> souls were traded and
> humanity was tested,
> to the brutal claws of colonization, which
> sought to suppress and
> reshape her essence,
> her suffering has been profound. Yet,
> from these depths of darkness,
> there emerges
> a profound medicine,
> one that
> the world deeply needs.

In
the resilience of her children,
torn from their homelands
yet rising in distant shores, there is
a testament to
the human spirit's indomitable will.
Their stories,
echoing through time,
remind us that
even when humanity
is stripped of its freedoms,
its spirit cannot be chained.
Their
melodies,
rhythms,
and dances,
birthed from the pain of separation, have
enriched global culture,
showing us that even in
suffering,
beauty can be born.

From
the heartache of apartheid, where
skin color became a yoke
and brother
was pitted against brother, came
a lesson
 in forgiveness and reconciliation.
The world
watched, rapt, as
Africa showed
that love could heal
the deepest of divides,
that unity could emerge from
 the ashes of hatred.
The likes of Mandela became
not just Africa's heroes but
beacons for humanity,
exemplifying that
true power lies
not in suppression,
but in upliftment.

Furthermore, Africa's struggles with
famine,
war,
and disease have yielded
stories
of community,
of neighbors supporting neighbors,
of strangers becoming family.
In a world
often fragmented by borders and differences,
Africa's experiences serve as
a reminder
of our shared humanity,
of our collective responsibility to
heal,
nurture,
and grow.

But perhaps the deepest medicine Africa offers
is the wisdom of perspective.
In the face of adversity, there emerges
a clarity,
a realization
of what truly matters.
Her pain
teaches us
to value life,
to cherish relationships,
to respect nature,
 and to seek harmony.
It pushes us to question our
definitions of
success,
wealth,
and progress.

In essence, Africa's suffering has
served as a crucible,
refining
and reshaping
not only
the continent but the entire world.
Her tears
have watered seeds of change,
her wounds
have birthed movements of liberation,
and her heartbeats,
despite every ordeal,
have sung songs of hope,
 unity,
and love.
Through her trials, Africa
gifts the world
a deep medicine – a balm
of resilience,
a tonic
of unity,
and a salve
of hope.

'griot'

Modern Griots,
you
who dance between the lines
of ancient and now,
painting with bold strokes
the vibrant canvas of our Africa.
in your hands,
the past
is reborn,
whispers becoming roars,
and every note
you play,
every word
you weave,
is the heartbeat
of a continent alive
with dreams
and memories.

you
are the storytellers,
keepers of our flame,
in the art you create
lies
the power
to change,
to challenge,
to charm.
with every melody,
every brushstroke,
every narrative,
you
redefine
what it means to be African
 in a world
ever shrinking,
ever expanding.

your songs
are more than music;
they are
the voice
of our cities,
echoing through streets paved
with hope
and history.

        your stories
        are not just tales;
        they are
        reflections
        of our soul,
        mirrors
        held up to a world
        that often forgets to look.

in your art,
Africa speaks,
bold
and unapologetic,
a symphony
of colors
and sounds,
telling the world who we are,
who we have been,
and who we will become.

modern Griots,
carry
 this legacy,
this responsibility,
with
the joy
and gravity it deserves.
for in
your words,
in your art,
lies
the future of our continent,
a future as bright
and boundless
as the African sky.
so rise,
create,
inspire,
for in your hands
rests
the story of Africa,
waiting
to be told.

'villainy'

There exists an elusive yet pervasive antagonist
in the vast, multifaceted narrative of Africa,
a continent of paradoxes
painted in vivid hues of diversity.

This foe,
unlike the colonial oppressors of the past
or the corrupt leaders in media's glare,
is far more insidious,
for it dwells
within
the very psyche
of societies and individuals alike.

It is
the twin specter of
hopelessness and
apathy,
a villain
not of flesh and bone
but of
spirit and mind.

This adversary
does not announce itself
with the
boom of a cannon
or the
slash of a sword.
Instead, it creeps in
silently,
like a shadow at dusk,
seeping into the hearts and minds
of people,
eroding the foundations of hope
and the will to act.
It is a force that turns
potential
into stagnation,
aspiration
into resignation,
and vibrant dreams
into
faded memories.

Hopelessness,
the first of this diabolic duo,
is born from a history scarred
by exploitation
and disappointment.
It whispers a deceptive narrative,
suggesting that change
is a distant fantasy,
unattainable
and elusive.
This voice of despair speaks in the language
of past failures
and present difficulties,

painting a future
devoid of possibility.
It breeds a sense of futility, a belief that
efforts to improve are but drops
in an ocean of entrenched challenges.

Apathy,
its sinister twin,
follows in the wake of
hopelessness.
Where the fire of passion and
the desire for change once burned,
apathy leaves a cold,
numbing indifference.
It manifests in a
collective shrug at corruption,
a blind eye to injustice,
and a deaf ear to the cries of the marginalized.
This detachment is not a lack of concern,
but a defense mechanism
against the relentless tide
of challenges
perceived as insurmountable.

Together, hopelessness and apathy
create a vicious cycle,
a feedback loop
that stifles progress
and dims the light of innovation
and change.
In the face of these adversaries,
initiatives falter,
reforms stall,
and the vibrant mosaic of African potential
is left unweaved.

Yet,
as with all great narratives,
there is a counterforce
to this villainy.
It lies
in the resilient spirit
of the African people,
a spirit that has endured
through centuries of upheaval and transformation.
The antidote to hopelessness and apathy
is found
in the stories
of individuals
and communities who,
despite the odds,
continue to strive for a better future.

It is seen
in the young entrepreneur in Lagos, who,
against economic uncertainties,
launches a startup
with the dream of solving local problems.
It is evident
in the community leader in Rwanda, who
fosters reconciliation and peace
in a land
once torn by unimaginable strife.
It is present
in the voices of activists across the continent,
who refuse
to be silenced in their fight
for justice and equality.

These stories, often overlooked,
form the undercurrent of
a continent on the move,
a narrative of resilience and hope
that defies the grip
of our intangible villains.
They remind us that
the future of Africa is not
predetermined
or doomed
to a cycle of despair and inaction.
Rather, it is a canvas
upon which a new generation,
armed with t
he lessons of the past
and the innovations of the present,
can paint
a future
of their own making.

The true battle
for Africa's future
is not against external foes but against
the internal specters
of hopelessness
and apathy.
The victory over these villains
lies in
reigniting
the flame of hope
and fostering a culture of
proactive engagement.
For in the heart of every African,
there lies the potential
to be
an agent of change,
a builder of the future,
and a conqueror of the unseen adversaries
that threaten the continent's progress.

'self-compassion'

As Africa looks back,
let it do so
with the understanding that
its history,
no matter how tumultuous,
is the crucible in which
its identity
has been forged.

>As it looks forward,
>let it do so
>with the courage to imagine
>a future
>where every child
>born under its sun
>can write their own story,
>free
>from the shadows of the past,
>their hearts
>unburdened,
>their spirits
>unbound.

As Africa stands
on the brink of tomorrow,
there is
a whisper of hope
 that is rooted
not in the innocence of untested dreams,
but in the gritty reality
of a dreamer
well acquainted with disappointment,
yet daring to dream still.
This future is not
an escape
but a dialogue with the past,
where the lessons
of yesteryears
 become
the stepping stones
for the triumphs of tomorrow.

Along the way, we hear
a call
to self-reflection,
an invitation
for Africa
to face its dark past
head-on,
accept its ghosts,
and come out the other side
proud
of its resiliency
and the hardships it has overcome.

The African experience
is not a flat, homogeneous story
but rather a montage
 of varied
and intricate
narratives.
It is a story about how diverse people
can be powerful,
how many different voices
can sing
the same song of the continent,
but in
their own unique ways
and with
their own distinct stories.

The story is a patchwork weaving
spun
from the threads of history,
where each strand
relates a story of shackles and strength,
of a continent's unwavering will
to survive
the ebb and flow of
rule and history.

This land, with its scars and wisdom,
speaks of a past
both haunting and heroic.
Its history, a labyrinth
where paths of light and darkness intertwine,
tells of journeys taken in chains
and roads paved
with indomitable will.
Here, in this reflection, is a call
not for bitterness, but for
a clear-eyed gaze of
self-compassion.
For within these tales of oppression
lies the testament to
an unquenchable spirit,
a spirit that refused to be
defined
by its oppressors.

> In this delicate balance of memory and hope lies
> Africa's true challenge
> and greatest promise:
> forging a future that honors the past
> as a rich,
> complex legacy,
> a wellspring of wisdom
> for future generations.

'mother tongue'

From the rolling rhythms of Swahili,
To the lyrical lilt of Amharic,
In the click and cadence of Xhosa,
To the sonorous tones of Yoruba,
wisdom we seek.

Each tongue,
a unique melody,
a distinct echo of ages old,
A testament to the beauty in diversity,
 in stories bold.

Zulu chants rise like the sun over savannah plains,
Igbo words weave tales of moons, of joys and pains.
Hausa, with its gentle flow, like a river's song,
And the vibrant energy of Shona, where spirits belong.

Each language,
a universe,
A manifold of culture,
They speak of kings and warriors,
of ancient rites, Of harvest moons,
rainy seasons,
and starlit nights.

In the market's buzz, a thousand dialects blend,
 In the elder's tales, the old and new transcend.
Children's laughter, in many tongues,
a chorus of delight,
In every language,
 the story of life takes flight.

But these voices now, in the winds of time,
grow faint,
As modern tides rise,
with their monochrome paint.
Let us not forget the richness in this linguistic sea,
The beauty of diversity,
of identity,
of history.
For in each African language, there's wisdom
deep and vast,
A bridge
to our ancestors,
a link
to our past.
So let us cherish
these tongues,
these precious sounds,
In them,
the heart of Africa,
eternally resounds.

'male benefactor'

African man,
benefactor of legacy,
guardian
of our essence
where
spirit
and purpose
intertwine
with passion.

Consider him as a child,
his feet
tapping on
the fertile soils that
gave birth to humanity.
His laughter,
echoing the rhythms
of ancient drums,
a promise, a foretaste of
stories
that will shape
the future.
 Each gaze, each awe,
paints dreams on the Serengeti and
dances with the winds that
once carried
the voices of ancestral kings.

Witness the young warrior,
his strength
coursing
through veins rich in heritage.
His stride,
reminiscent
of ancient migrations, carries
stories of valor,
love,
and sacrifice.
He embodies the resilience
of a continent that has
endured,
thrived,
and bestowed gifts upon the world,
as he stands
against
the backdrop of Kilimanjaro or the expanse of the Sahara.
His spirit
shines forth like a beacon,
 illuminating
paths both
remembered and unknown.

Respect the father,
the bearer of life,
the protector.
Futures are nurtured in
the cradle of his arms, and
generations find their bearings in
the wisdom of his words. He is
the river,
ever-flowing,
nourishing lands and souls alike.
His legacy,
infused with
Timbuktu's ancient teachings and
the Nile's timeless wisdom, is
a testament to
love
that transcends time.

    Honor the elder,
    whose skin,
    etched with stories
    and time, becomes
    a living collection of history.
    His eyes,
    repositories of eons, hold
    stories that span
    the plains of Maasai Mara,
    Johannesburg's bustling vibrancy, and
    the mystic alleys of Marrakech.
    He is the bridge,
    the liaison,
    connecting the past's glory
    with the future's
    potential.

An African man is
a multitude of experiences
an alchemy of essence,
from the beauty of Dakar's coast
to the rich culture of Addis Ababa.
In him,
epochs converge,
traditions rejuvenate,
and
the pulse of Africa
finds its rhythm.
Every gesture,
every utterance,
every reflection
is a tribute
to a lineage unparalleled.

> He is
> the griot of modern times,
> the custodian of ancient secrets,
> the benefactor to a world
> often unaware
> of its own indebtedness.

To celebrate him is
to comprehend the breadth of the
sky,
the profundity of roots, and t
he essence of time itself.
For in the African man
lies
the heart of humanity,
the soul of the earth,
the benefactor of legacies
that will
forever
shape our cosmos.

'Letter from An Ancestor'

umAfrika wam,

> From out here in the great unknown, where time does not matter,
> above the noise and lights of your current day,
> I, your ancestor,
> with eyes that have seen the fire and the rain,
> Watch over you,
> feeling every joy, every pain.

I have walked old paths where ancient spirits danced.
I have listened to the wind and been captivated by its songs.
Now, from this timeless place, I look upon you and see,
A continent wrestling with its past, striving to break free.

> Each step you take towards a bright new horizon,
> I worry that you lose touch with what makes you unique.
> Where are the tales we told,
> the songs we once sung?
> The stories that echoed
> in every mother tongue?

Yet, even in my deepest despair,
I find a glimmer of hope,
For I see in you tenacity and a wide range of abilities.
Your youth,
marching forward, bear in their souls,
A piece of our legacy,
our stories, our goals.

>I yearn to speak, to share wisdom from our time,
>To remind you of our struggles, our mountains yet to climb.
>Because within every choice, every path that you tread,
>Echoes a piece of our history, words left unsaid.

Times evolve, and the world wears a new guise,
But my love, Africa, you are the prize.
From this realm, where past and future collide,
Know that my spirit, my essence, is forever by your side.

>Embrace the old with the new, let them intertwine,
>For in this dance of eras, both stories must shine.
>Always remember, as you carve your own run,
>Our legacy, your journey, are forever one.

With eternal love,
Ukhokho Wakho.

"Progeny": An Ancestral Mother's Musings

The winds of Sahel murmur secrets in my ears,
and the rivers of Congo hum lullabies of tales yet to unfold.
My soul marvels at the beauty and tragedy of existence. I muse upon the future of my children's children, an endless lineage of souls borne from my womb.
How will you remember me, unborn ones?
Will you feel the echoes of my heartbeat in the rhythm of the drum?
Will you see my dreams in the twinkling constellations of the Saharan nights?
I hope that you carry forward the legacy of our shared stories, those whispered at nightfall and sung at daybreak.
From the pyramids of Giza to the bustling markets of Dar es Salaam, I've seen empires rise and civilizations bloom. But I've also witnessed the pain of chains, the cruelty of conquest, the darkness that sometimes clouds human hearts.
I want you to know both the agony and the ecstasy, my dear progeny, because it is in this duality that wisdom is forged.
I see you, future daughters, with eyes ablaze, challenging conventions and shattering the ceilings made of age-old prejudices. I see you, future sons, redefining strength, with compassion as your shield and understanding as your sword.
Yet, I also fear.
Your modern world's sirens beckon, with their shimmering illusions and hollow promises.

Will you forget the melodies of your ancestors in favor of the transient tunes of your today? Will the sacredness of the land, the respect for every creature, and the unity of communities become mere tales of a bygone era?
However, amidst these apprehensions, a hope burgeons.
For in every reflection upon the waters of Nile, in every gust of the Harmattan, in every dance step upon the red soils of our homeland, there remains an essence, an eternal spirit.
It is this spirit, this unbreakable connection to the roots, that I entrust to you.
May you traverse the globe, exploring its myriad wonders, but always feel the pull of home. May you face challenges with the resilience of the mountain and the adaptability of the river.
And as you move forward in time, remember that you are the dreams of countless generations, the culmination of hopes, sacrifices, and love beyond measure.

IV

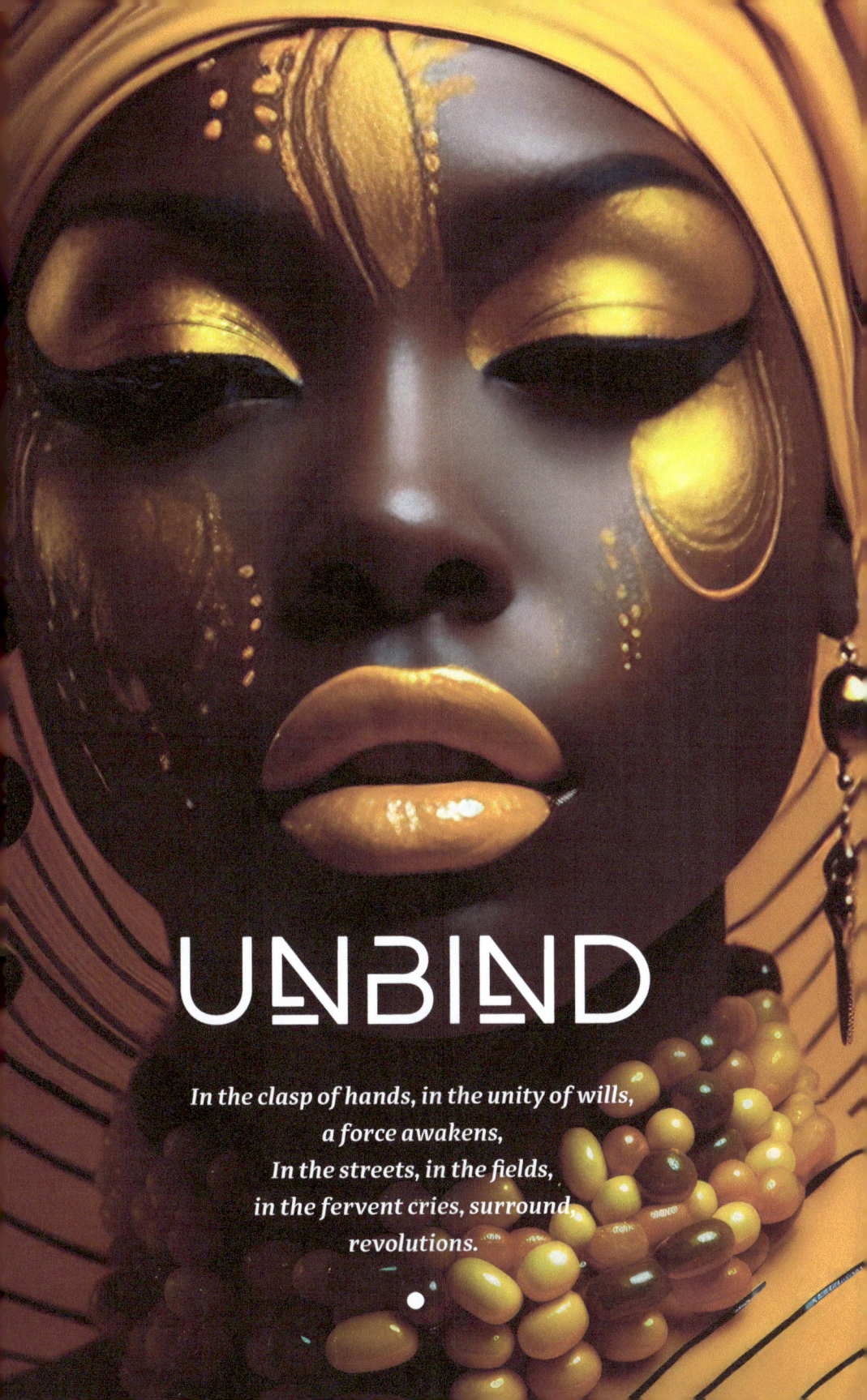

'defense'

A stone tablet
bearing the inscription "Defense" is buried
deep within Africa.
Its characters, etched by time and nature,
hold
the very soul and tumult of
a continent's perpetual confrontation with resistance.

Physically..., the continent is
etched by nature's own hand with defenses: vast plateaus,
unfathomable rainforests, and unyielding deserts.
These natural barriers, which once kept invaders at bay,
also became Africa's own cage.
The vastness protected, yet paradoxically isolated.
They shielded from outside foes, but also
confined the diverse tribes, sometimes
fueling discord from within.

Emotionally..., the African heart, vast and profound, has
known defense as a double-edged sword.
Songs of joy and
dances of celebration
have, for generations, acted as
barriers against
the weight of oppression and
the sting of colonization. But
behind the jubilant beats and rhythmic steps,
there lies
a shielded sorrow, denial,
a defense
against acknowledging wounds that still fester.

Mentally..., defense took the form of narratives.
In the face of colonizers' tales that
sought to diminish and distort, Africa
responded with
a torrent of stories,
tales,
and histories that
fiercely defended its essence.
But in this defensive act, were
there other truths left untold?
Were there lesser voices silenced in
the urgency to create a singular, resistant narrative?

Spiritually..., the most effective barrier against
existential despair in Africa was
its rich diversity of beliefs.
Belief in countless deities, ancestor spirits, and
complex rituals granted solace and intention. Yet,
the introduction
of foreign faiths muddled these waters, offering
both spiritual expansion and, at times,
a loss of essence.

Drawing upon
this passionate critique, the stone
meditates deeply on defense.
It does not merely ask, but rather
demands introspection:
In our act of defending, what
essence of ourselves do
we retain, and what
do we inadvertently leave behind?

Defense, as Africa has known it, is
neither purely a savior
nor a captor.
It is the
complex dance
between preservation and progression,
between the self and the other.

The stone, though silent,
resonates with
the echoes
of a continent's soul,
forever meditating on
its place within
the vast fabric of
humanity
and existence.

'memories of revolution'

She is a continent both ancient
and eternally young,
her vast narrative carries a past
marked by the harsh influence of colonialism,
the fierce spirit of revolutions,
the bittersweet symphony of independence.

    This story depicts wounds
    and victories of many countries; each chapter
    is a multifaceted triumph and tragedy, of
    hopes dashed and
    hopes resurrected.

Consider
each nation representing a
distinct thread that is dynamic and
brimming with vitality.
From the pyramids of Egypt to the Cape of Good Hope,
from the golden sands of the Sahara to the lush rainforests of the Congo,
the continent thrums
with the memories of its colonial past,
a time when foreign powers
etched their desires and designs upon its vast canvas.

The colonial era, a time of contradictions,
saw the reshaping of Africa's destiny
by hands other than its own.
There was plunder
and exploitation, yes, but also
the inadvertent knitting together of nations,
the unintended creation of
new identities.
In this crucible of foreign rule,
the seeds of rebellion were sown,
watered by the tears
of those who longed for freedom.

>   Ah, the revolutions! Each
>   a story unto itself,
>   a drama rich with heroes
>   and villains, triumphs
>   and tragedies.

Kenya's Mau Mau uprising,
a brutal yet
poignant struggle;
Algeria's war of independence,
a tale of
resistance and relentless
pursuit of self-determination;
Ghana, under Nkrumah's visionary leadership,
lighting the path to freedom
without bloodshed—these were
but the opening acts
of a continent-wide
quest for
liberation.

The attainment of independence, however,
 was not the end of the story, but
the beginning of
a new, complex narrative.
Nations,
once bound by
the shackles of colonialism,
found themselves at the
crossroads of history,
tasked with charting their own course.
This era, a kaleidoscope
of hope and uncertainty,
saw the emergence
of new challenges – the
 building of nations from
the fractured legacies
of colonial rule.

Consider Nigeria,
with its array of ethnicities
and religions,
striving to find unity in diversity;
Zimbabwe,
emerging from the
shadow of Rhodesian rule, grappling with
the complexities of self-governance;
South Africa, a phoenix rising from
the ashes of apartheid, embarking
on a journey towards
reconciliation and equality.
Each nation,
a microcosm of the larger African story—a narrative
of resilience,
of dreams reimagined,
of futures redefined.

Africa's rich mosaic of experiences serves
as a reminder that
the past, no matter how turbulent,
is a stepping stone to
a future
yet to be written.
 a tale of
perseverance a
nd change rather than
of victimization
or defeat.
in the heart of every
African nation lies not just
the echoes of a colonial legacy, but
the resounding beat of a
continent rising,
resilient and proud, its narrative f
orever unfolding
in the hands
of its people.

'stifle': A Labyrinth of Reflection

The corridors and alcoves stretched infinitely,
creating a vast and ageless library where
each bookshelf brims with tales of the world.

> Here, a lone traveler stumbled upon
> an enigmatic volume titled "Stifle".
> The leather-bound book, aged and worn,
> spoke of a concept deeply intertwined with
> the fabric of African life.

The first page detailed a vast savannah,
where the horizons
blended seamlessly with the sky, suggesting infinity.
Yet, as the traveler read further,
he realized that
this expansive vista was but an illusion.

> The very air seemed thickened,
> heavy, charged with an unseen weight.
> Animals roamed, but
> their strides seemed muted, their roars muffled.
> The vastness wasn't freeing; it was
> a silent oppressor.

Progressing through the tome, the narrative
shifted to ancient cities built of
sun-baked clay and adorned
with symbols, both mundane and mystical.
The alleys were alive with
merchants, mystics, and minstrels.

> But amidst this bustling life,
> there lingered an intangible haze.
> The streets, though wide,
> seemed narrow, and the high walls,
> though protective, seemed imprisoning.

This concept of "stifle" was not
limited to physical manifestations.
The book spoke of oral traditions,
tales told under moonlit skies,
where the line between
the mundane and the magical was blurred.

> Yet, even in these tales, there were stories that
> remained unsaid, characters lost in the annals of time,
> and truths too intricate or painful to be verbalized.

The volume hinted at languages lost,
dialects diluted,
and voices silenced.
It pondered on memories suppressed,
histories rewritten,
and identities reshaped.

Amidst the maze of ideas, the voyager
noticed a consistent theme or pattern:
a wealth of knowledge and potential that is
frequently obscured by
internal anxieties and outside influences.

Towards the book's end,
the narrative became self-referential.
The traveler read of a man, much like himself,
wandering through an endless library,
discovering this very volume.
The boundaries between reader and narrative,
between reality and fiction, began to blur.
And as the last page turned,
the traveler was left with more questions than answers.

> Was this "stifle"
> an inherent aspect of African life?
> Or was it a lens, a perspective?
> Perhaps, the labyrinth's concept was
> not to find an exit
> but to understand the maze.

Could it be that "stifle", in its omnipresence,
was not a statement of oppression
but a challenge?
A call to recognize these moments of restraints,
to face them, and to transcend?

> Was the labyrinth, with its myriad reflections,
> prompting each wanderer
> to see the many facets of stifling – not as barriers,
> but as the very elements that define the journey?

As he placed the book back on the shelf,
the corridors of the library
seemed to shift, almost imperceptibly.
The weight of "stifle" lingered, urging him to ponder,
to seek, and perhaps,
in understanding, to transcend.

When one considers what "stifle" means in
the context of African life,
it is clear that the real maze is
not found in the records
but rather in the mind,
where each idea and reflection becomes
a path
that can lead to
either confinement
or
liberation.

The "Good African": A Critique

When the world speaks of Africa, its descriptions veer wildly between the shimmering mirages of its past and the burdensome shadows of its present. A continent simultaneously caught in the fierce embrace of time and timeless oblivion.

However, before we cast judgment from our own internalized perspectives, or bow to the critiques of the external world, we must embark upon an introspective journey. Only then can we define, with utmost clarity, the essence of the "Good African."

Our past is the luminous tale of kingdoms and empires, the seat of wisdom where ancient scholars once thronged, the cradle of humankind, and the canvas where nature painted its grandest landscapes.

But time's relentless march has not been kind, and as the sands shifted, so did the tales. Instead of the illustrious account of Carthage, Mali, and the Great Zimbabwe, we are confronted with narratives of war, famine, corruption, and the irrevocable scars of colonization.

As we highlight the sufferings and resilience of the marginalized, we must also shine a light on the internal divisions that have been our Achilles' heel. Ethnic rivalry, corruption at the hands of our own, and the surrender of our resources to foreign powers are tales we must confront with gritted teeth and open hearts.

Yet, Africa is not just the sum of its pain or the catalog of its missteps. Within its vastness lies a mosaic of diverse cultures, each unique, yet bound by the same thread of indomitable spirit and boundless potential.

What then, is the "Good African"?

The Good African understands that our legacy is a double-edged sword. It is both a reservoir of pride and a reservoir of lessons.

The Good African neither dwells in the past nor dismisses it. Instead, they learn from it, take what is useful, and propel forward.
Externally, the world has often defined Africa through the lenses of pity, fear, or sheer ignorance. But the Good African listens, not to be submissive, but to differentiate between constructive criticism and prejudiced disdain. Where the critiques are grounded in truth, there is a readiness to change. Where they stem from ignorance, there is patience to educate.
To the world that has oftentimes misunderstood us, the Good African extends an invitation – to witness the rebirth of a continent. To be part of an epoch where history doesn't repeat, but rather, refines itself.
In this spirit of introspection, let us, the sons and daughters of Africa, strive to be the embodiment of this 'Good African'. Not to appease external critics or fit into their narrow definitions, but to fulfill our potential, realize our dreams, and retake our rightful place in the annals of world history.
The sun may have set, but it is also destined to rise again.

V

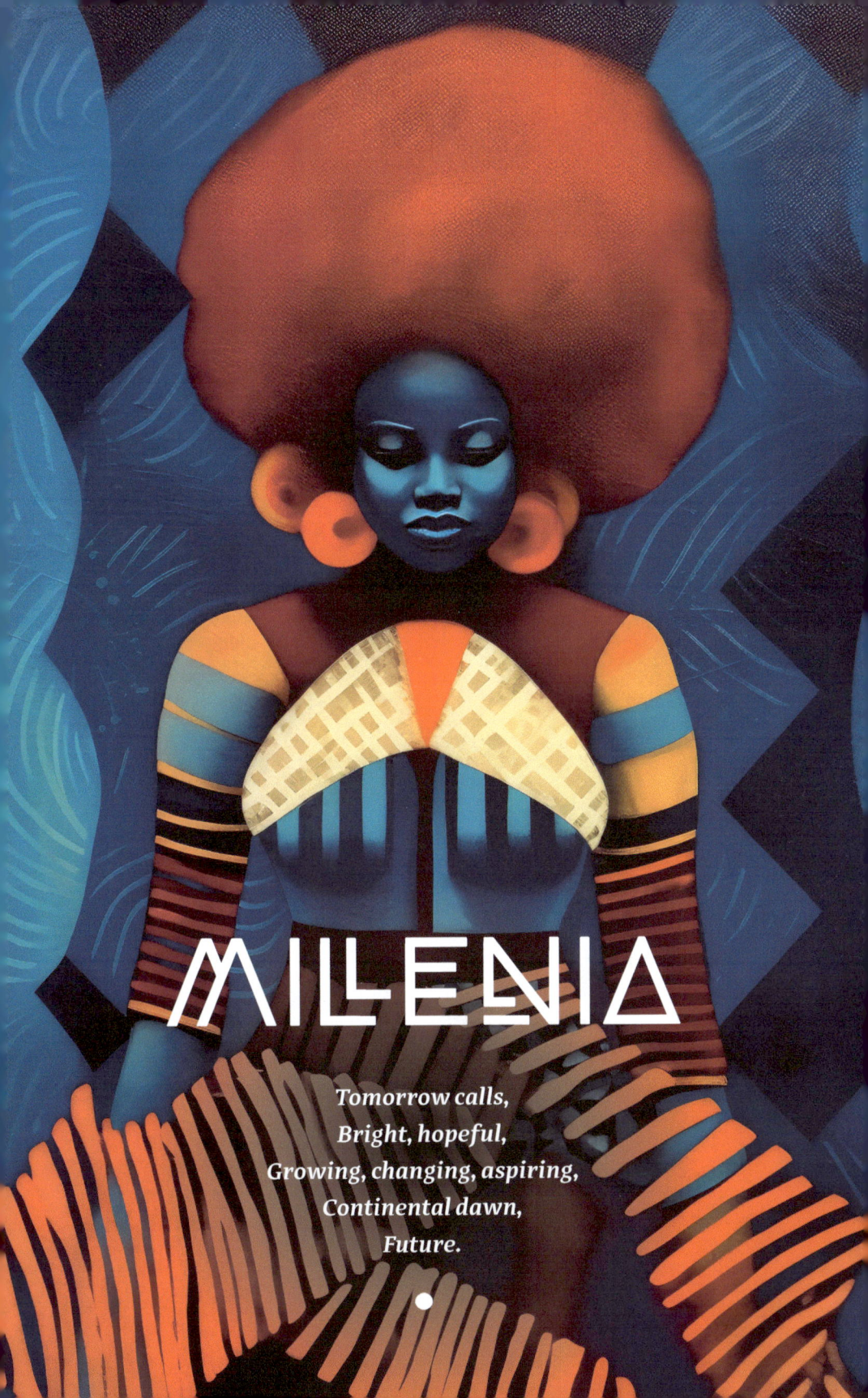

'manifesto'

Across
the golden Sahara
One finds a timeless narrative.
It's not just a chronicle of dates and events,
but a passionate testament
shaped by countless souls over millennia.

>From Africa, the heartland,
> there emerges a rhythm.
> It's not just audible; it's palpable.
> It tells tales of triumphs and tribulations,
> of boundless joy and deep-rooted pain.
> This land, the cradle of humankind,
> has seen the dawn of civilizations,
> the rise and fall of empires,
> and the relentless spirit of its people.

Yet history,
in its many renditions,
has often been unjust.

> It has overshadowed Africa's
> gleaming contributions with tales of subjugation and
> exploitation.
> But hidden beneath this veil of misrepresentation are
> stories of gold, not just of the mineral, but
> of rich cultures,
> diverse languages,
> and unparalleled heritage.

Kings, queens, warriors, and wise sages once walked these lands,
leaving indelible footprints on time's vast canvas.
From the pinnacle of pyramids
to the scholarly treasures of Timbuktu,
our legacy is profound,
intricate,
and defiant in the face of attempts to cage it.

> The irony of history is that
> this continent, so rich in essence, has
> been portrayed as lesser, its achievements
> often diminished or forgotten.

But the undying spirit
of Africa and its people persists,
resilient and unwavering,
a beacon
that cannot be extinguished.
To the generations yet to come,
 here's an earnest appeal.
Seek freedom,
not just from tangible chains,
but from the shackles of
ignorance and self-doubt.

For in the true understanding of oneself, one discovers the most profound liberation.

> This manifesto speaks of hope,
> determination,
> and an unyielding light.
> It is a declaration to the world:
> Africa's progeny,
> bearing the weight of timeless legacies,
> will forever illuminate the path forward.
> In their journey,
> they carry with them
> a wealth of stories
> and the promise of
> a brighter,
> resplendent future.

'bonds & visions'

Africa stands as a land of paradoxes and enigmas.
It's a place where the soil
whispers tales older than the mountains
and the rivers
carry secrets deep into the heart of the ocean.
Here,
dreams intertwine with reality
and time dances with memory.

> Imagine, if you will, a tree
> with roots made
> of golden sunsets and silver dawns.
> Its branches stretch outward,
> not towards the sky, but
> into the very fabric of dreams.
> Each leaf, a memory, each fruit, a story.

This is Africa,
not just a continent,
but an ethereal entity, breathing life into every crack and crevice
of the universe.

> Giraffes
> with necks as long as tales told by grandmothers reach for stars,
> sipping stardust and humming lullabies that rock the moon to sleep.
> Elephants,
> with tusks made of condensed clouds,
> roam vast savannahs, their footsteps creating rhythmic patterns
> that become the heartbeat of the earth.

However, there are elements of reality and perception within this strange fabric.
Bonds of brotherhood,
woven from shared histories and collective memories, tie its people together.
Chains of past transgressions,
though heavy,
become the very anchors that ground dreams into aspirations,
 turning pain into power,
scars into stars.

> From the Saharan dunes, where time itself gets lost,
> to the rich jungles of Congo, where every shadow holds a mystery,
> the bonds of Africa stretch and coil,
> connecting not just its lands,
> but also its souls.

The pyramids, ancient as the universe itself,
are not just tombs of pharaohs,
 but portals into alternate dimensions,
where past, present, and future merge into a kaleidoscope of existence.

> Seas, not just of water
> but of emotions,
> crash upon its shores.
> The waves, imbued with the laughter and tears of generations,
> bring tales from distant realms,
> while the sands on the beach capture imprints,
> not of feet,
> but of souls,
> preserving them for eternity.

Bonds are more than just connections in this dreamscape;
they are the very threads that weave life itself.
Africa,
with her surreal heart and soul,
stands testament to the enduring power of these bonds and visions,
echoing through time and space,
a symphony of love,
resilience,
and hope.

'millennia: Africa apologia'

She has persevered
for millennia,
her spirit unbroken, her voice unquenchable.
Yet,
when the world gathers,
when high tables are set
and decisions are made,
her seat
is frequently misplaced.
Why?

    Consider
    the annals of time.
    Before
    the first ship sailed,
    before
    the first empire rose,
    Africa was.
    She was
    the cradle, the genesis, the beginning of beginnings.
    Her stories
    are the world's first tales,
    her songs
    the original symphonies.

Millennia have seen her give,
endlessly,
selflessly,
to the world.
Her soil birthed humanity,
her heart birthed culture.
Is that
not seat-worthy?

        When the world thirsted for knowledge,
        Africa's ancient libraries in Timbuktu
        quenched curious souls.
        When civilizations sought guidance,
        they turned to her pyramids, her sculptures, her age-old wisdom.
        She taught the world
        to speak,
        to count,
        to dream.
        Millennia
        of contribution,
        millennia
        of illumination.
        Does that not demand recognition?

Yet,
when borders were drawn, often not by her hand,
and resources plundered, not for her benefit,
she was told
to wait,
to learn,
to catch up.
But catch up to what?
To millennia of her own teachings?
To her own endless wealth of spirit and resource?

>This is not defiance;
>it is a call to memory,
>a plea for justice.

In her valleys and mountains,
in her rivers and plains,
lie lessons the world needs now more than ever.
Of unity,
of harmony,
of respect for the earth and each other.
In her dances,
her songs,
her tales,
lie the solutions to a world fragmented,
a world forgetting.

>Millennia of healing,
>millennia of connection.
>Should she not lead the discourse?

It is not defiance to demand rightful space.
 It is not audacity to ask for acknowledgment.
It is a call to the world to remember,
to recognize,
to realize.
Africa is not just a part of the world's story;
she IS the story.
Millennia stand witness.

So,
when the world hosts its
high tables,
its
grand discussions,
its
vision for the future,
let it remember
the millennia.
Let it remember
Africa.
For in sidelining her,
the world forgets its own roots,
its essence,
its true north.

>   Africa does not plead for a seat.
>   She reclaims it.
>   Because Africa is
>   timeless and eternal,
>   she deserves her proper place
>   in the grand scheme of existence,
>   where millennia
>   speak
>   louder than mere moments.

'god of death': Africa defiant

In the land where earth sings its birth song,
Under
the heavy gaze
of a sun that refuses to blink,
Calamity descended,
wearing
the mask of a god of death,
There, where the Baobabs stand like wise elders in congregation.

> Yet, Africa,
> in her timeless splendor,
> Turned her face,
> chiseled by centuries,
> wrought with resilience,
> And dared to challenge this phantom deity,
> With a voice echoing
> from the Sahara's vastness to Kilimanjaro's peak.

"god of death, do you not know?
We, who danced under the canopy of stars,
Who whispered secrets to the winds,
Have faced your kind before."

"Colonial specters,
wars that bleed into rivers,
Droughts that whispered despair,
Yet,
from the Nile's nurturing arms
to the Cape of Good Hope,
We stood,
unbroken,
unbowed."

    "god of death, what have you but ephemeral power?
    Our spirits,
    wrapped in tales spun by ancient griots,
    Resist,
    persist,
    insist on life,
    For in every African heart, defiance is a flame that never dies."

Look then upon the colorful markets of Marrakech,
The joyful dances in the streets of Lagos,
The poets who dream in Johannesburg's embrace,
And know,
oh calamity,
you face a continent undeterred.

    "god of death, take heed and retreat,
    For Africa,
    in her grand majesty of tribes and tongues,
    Knows the rhythm of life,
    the pulse of survival,
    And in her song,
    even gods
    can be defeated."

VI

'signs from heaven': Africa's Humble Brag

Africa,
true to her nature,
does not proclaim her greatness loudly.

> Instead,
> she hints subtly
> at the heavenly markers in the sky
> that define her essence.

Here, nature's canvas reveals stories of heritage,
dignity,
and unyielding power.

> In the sprawling stretches where sky and land meet,
> Africa stands as a testament,
> adorned with the contrasts of light and obscurity.

If one were to draw closer,
they might see Africa
not just as a continent
but as a character.

> She grapples with her identity
> in a world that often misunderstands her,
> defining her through narrow lenses.
> Yet, through her understated revelations,
> Africa communicates her value.

Consider the Nile,
its meandering path nurturing civilizations.
Isn't its course a divine message,
suggesting that life's journey,
though winding, is purposeful and profound?

      The vast Sahara, too,
      with its sea of sands,
      might be seen as a heavenly metaphor.
      Its daunting vastness is a reminder
      that even the most arduous challenges
      are sprinkled with opportunities,
      each grain representing potential
      waiting to be uncovered.

Then there's the Serengeti,
a pulsing, living, dynamic web
showcasing the ebb and flow of existence.
The Great Migration it hosts is not just a spectacle;
it's a testament
to the rhythms of life
and rebirth,
orchestrated by forces beyond comprehension.

      But beyond these natural wonders,
      isn't Africa's truest celestial marker her people?

Their narratives,
melodies,
and shared joys
resonate with the harmonies of a universe
that knows
both sorrow
and celebration.

Yet, Africa,
ever graceful,
never brandishes these gifts with conceit.
She merely exists,
allowing the signs
to articulate their truths.

>	The signs from Heaven aren't just her hallmarks;
>	they serve as an invitation for the world to look deeper,
>	to move past mere perceptions,
>	and to engage with the symphony of history,
>	nature,
>	and spirit
>	that Africa offers.

'arise'

"Arise, Africa, for your light has come,
and the glory of the Creator beams upon you.
While darkness may cover other lands and clothe peoples in despair,
upon you,
the Divine light shines,
and His luminance is seen upon you."

    Gaze upon the horizon,
    O Land of Origin, and see!
    Your sons and daughters,
        those taken from you and those who chose distant lands,
    now return.
    They come from afar,
    carried by modern vessels of steel
    and by wings that soar the sky,
    they are magnetized by the soulful pull of their ancestral home.

Lift your eyes and look around,
O Continent of Origins!
Wild beasts,
symbols of nations and powers,
gather around you,
bringing gold and incense,
proclaiming the tales of your greatness.
The world will bear witness to the bounty of your shores,
the wealth of your soil, the spirit of your people.

The age-old Baobab trees stand tall,
and the endless savannah stretches forth
as silent testimonies of time passed and promises fulfilled.
The rivers that have nourished civilizations,
from the Nile to the Niger,
will shimmer with hope,
bringing forth life in abundance.

> Gone are the days of oppression,
> O Land of Endurance!
> The yokes of colonization,
> the chains of slavery,
> the scars of apartheid—they shall be but memories,
> testimonies of resilience.

No more shall you be termed "Forsaken,"
nor your lands called "Barren."
Instead, you shall be termed "My Delight,"
and your lands "United,"
for the Creator delights in you
and has taken you as His own.

> Though you were once the last,
> now you shall be foremost,
> a beacon for nations.
> Kings will be your foster fathers,
> and queens your nurturers.
> They will bow down before you,
> recognizing the spiritual wealth
> and divine purpose placed within your borders.

Rejoice, Africa!
For the sun shall no longer be your light by day,
nor will the brightness of the moon give you light;
instead, the Creator Himself will be your everlasting light,
and the days of your mourning shall come to an end.

> Now is your moment, Africa.
> A moment to ascend,
> to radiate,
> to claim the destiny woven into your very fabric.

As the world beholds your rise,
may they glimpse
the Divine's hand,
painting a masterpiece
across your boundless land.

'luminance'

Within the extensive fabric of history,
amidst majestic civilizations
and unbound periods of development,
an enduring
and unchanging beacon of light remains:
the African woman.

Behold the child,
the tender bud,
blossoming under the African sun.
With eyes wide as saucers, reflecting dreams as vast as the Sahara,
she is the promise of dawn,
 the whisper of tales yet untold.
Her laughter, pure and unbridled,
dances with the winds that have carried the songs of her ancestors.

Admire the maiden,
the blooming flower
in the heart of the savannah.
With grace that rivals the gazelle
and strength echoing the mighty elephant,
she treads paths both ancient and new.
Every step,
a rhythm,
every gesture,
a dance.
Her spirit, fierce and free,
is the heartbeat of the land,
a melody that resonates
from the peaks of Kilimanjaro to the depths of the Congo.

Revere the mother,
 the life-giver,
the nurturer.
With hands that have molded generations
and a heart that has known depths unfathomable,
she is the backbone of the continent.
Her wisdom,
distilled from the ages,
 is the nectar that feeds the souls of her children.
Her embrace,
as vast as the Nile,
is a haven,
a sanctuary,
a testament to love that knows no bounds.

Honor the matriarch,
the sage,
 the keeper of tales.
With eyes that gleam with the luminance of countless moons,
she holds stories
woven with the threads of time.
Her voice,
deep
and resonant,
carries echoes
of queens and warriors,
poets and dreamers.
She is the bridge between realms,
the guardian of legacies, the beacon that guides with a light undimmed.

From the bustling markets of Marrakech
to the serene shores of Zanzibar,
from the majestic plains of the Serengeti
to the bustling lanes of Lagos,
the African woman
is an embodiment
of artistry
and essence.
In her,
the past and the future converge,
traditions and innovations meld,
creating a symphony
of beauty unparalleled.

> Every braid tells a story,
> every rhythm of her feet
> sings of journeys traversed
> and horizons yet to be explored.
> In the curve of her smile,
> the hope
> of a continent shines,
> in the depth of her gaze,
> its soul
> is laid bare.
> She is the muse of griots,
> the inspiration of artists,
> the pulse of Africa.

>   To celebrate her
>   is to bask in luminance,
>   to dive deep
>   into an ocean of richness,
>   to touch
>   the very essence of life itself.

She is more
than just a character in the African story;
she is
its very essence,
its radiance,
its eternal glow.

>   In every stage,
>   in every style,
>   in every whisper of wind and rustle of leaves,
>   the African woman
>   shines,
>   illuminates,
>   and transcends.

VII

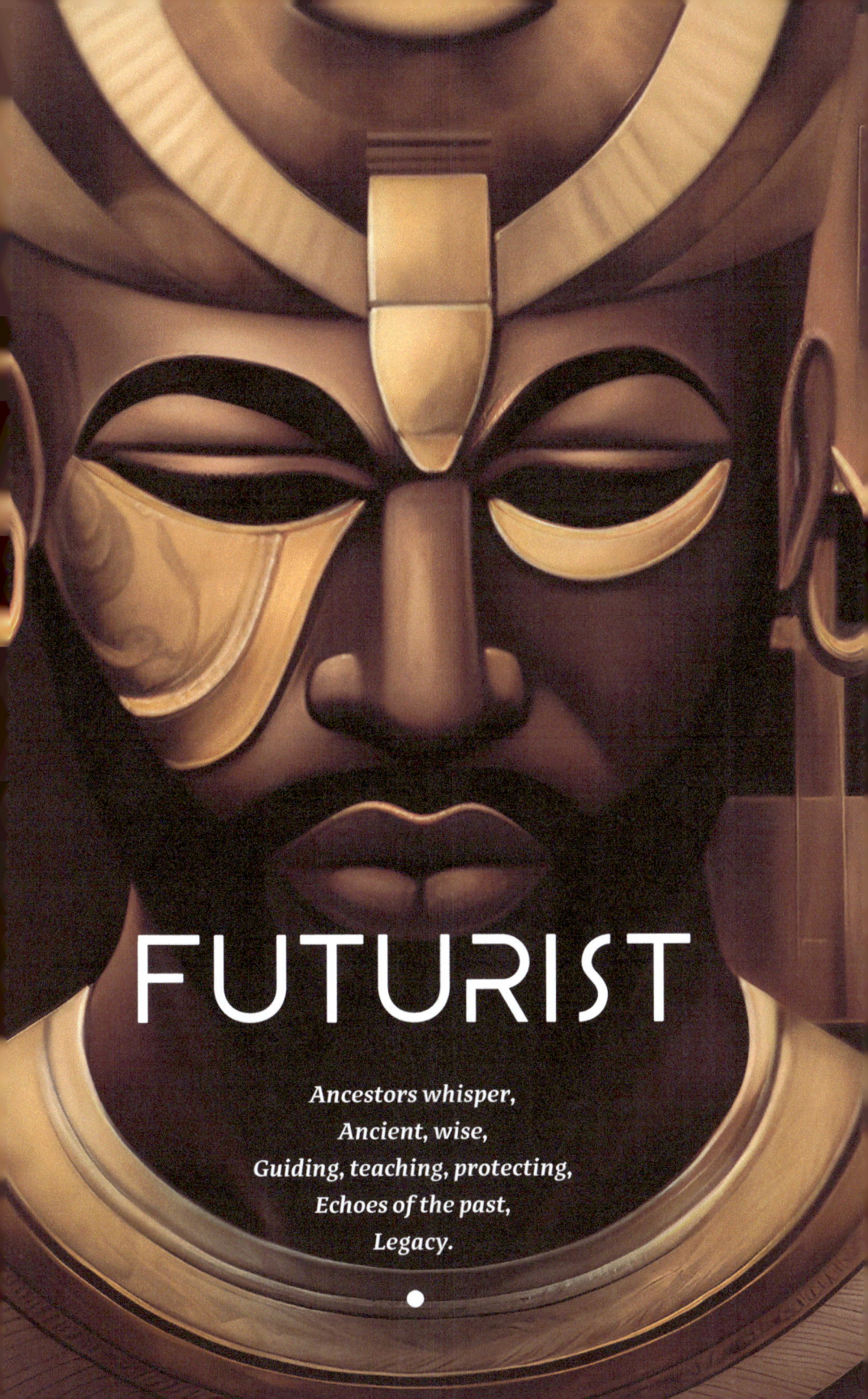

'antiquity: a futuristic descendant'

Gazing
from the far-off future,
where time has sculpted new myths
and galaxies have danced into new constellations,
I look back
at what was formerly referred to
as "cutting edge"
but is now
accepted as
"antiquity."

I pause
for reflection
on a world that was,
as seen
through my lens
of a world that is now.

Remember when humans
thought they were at
the pinnacle of innovation?
When
silicon chips were
their magic and
touchscreens their windows?
Those days of binary thought, virtual realities,
and digital frontiers without end?
From my vantage point, they now appear to be as old
as hieroglyphs on weathered stone
or quills on parchment.
A testament to an era of
discovery, but also
a humble reminder of
our ever-changing journey.

> The roaring engines that
> took mankind to the stars, the very stars
> we now call neighbors, are
> now artifacts of reverence.
> Those metallic birds that
> flew them
> across their blue planet, the web
> that connected minds and souls, the devices
> that held their world in
> the palm of their hands – all are now
> but echoes, resonating
> with a quaint charm from
> an era that, in its moment, believed it
> had touched eternity.

Just as they marveled at
the pyramids,
the ancient scrolls,
the first flicker of fire, I, too,
pause and reflect on t
heir marvels.
Their skyscrapers,
their satellites,
their boundless curiosity. But
while they saw endpoints, we see
stepping stones.
For isn't that the dance of progress? A continuum,
a relay where
one epoch's pinnacle becomes
the next's foundation.

Their dreams, bold and beautiful, painted in
the pixels
of their screens,
in the codes
of their machines, are
our legends.
We recount tales of
their first steps on distant moons,
their endeavors to harness the sun,
their quest to understand the very fabric of existence. Yet,
we smile, with tender affection, knowing
that our children will one day
look back at our now 'cutting edge'
as the antiquity
of their tomorrow.

Such is the
rhythm of time, the
ever-flowing
river of progress. Where
today's breakthroughs
are tomorrow's heirlooms, and
the future
always holds the promise
of realms unimagined.

    In this meditation, I do not
    merely marvel at the
    pace of evolution but find
    gratitude for
     every epoch,
    every age,
    every antiquity.
    For in each layer of the past,
    in the 'cutting edge' of every era,
     lies
    the heart of humanity,
    ever-beating,
    ever-dreaming,
    ever-reaching
    for the stars.

'revolution's song'

Freedom,
Loud, resounding,
Echoing, inspiring, liberating,
Melody of resilience and hope,
Anthem.

Voices,
Strong, united,
Singing, rising, proclaiming,
Harmony of liberation's dream,
Chorus.

Chains break,
Harsh, confining,
Shattering, releasing, freeing,
Rhythms of a new beginning,
Liberation.

Heroes,
Brave, relentless,
Fighting, enduring, achieving,
Ballad of the undaunted spirit,
Legacy.

Africa,
Proud, reborn,
Dreaming, thriving, evolving,
Symphony of enduring strength,
Song.

Lj Kareri

Lj Kareri is an award-winning Kenyan-born author, screenwriter and creative producer based in Los Angeles, CA.

She is founder and CEO of WhistleTree Media (www.whistletreemedia.com), a production company that develops film and television content, focusing on African original stories. Whistletree Media is currently signed to a multi-project development deal with leading global streaming company Netflix, for yet to be announced original drama series as part of their Africa-region 2025 slate.

Kareri is a passionate advocate for African culture and art, promoting it through digital design agency www.soulafrik.com and is committed to telling stories that reflect the diversity of the continent. She is also a strong advocate for global women and girls' rights and believes that they too should have a decisive voice in all aspects of society.

A graduate of the University of California, Los Angeles (UCLA) Professional Screenwriting Program (2011), she also holds a Bachelor of Science degree in Criminal Justice.

Contact / Literary Representative:
Sharon J. Wisnia | Producer / Manager
MoJo Global Arts | mojo.film
324 S. Beverly Dr., #185 | Beverly Hills, CA 90212
+1 310 430 5971 | sharon@mojo.film

www.ingramcontent.com/pod-product-compliance
Lightning Source LLC
Chambersburg PA
CBHW042054060526
44119CB00115B/291